SELE

INTERV

SELECTION
INTERVIEWING

by Christine Wright

The Industrial Society

First published 1973 by
The Industrial Society
Robert Hyde House
48 Bryanston Square
London W1H 7LN
Telephone 071 - 262 2401

Second edition, 1989
© *The Industrial Society, 1971, 1989*
Reprinted 1990, 1991

ISBN 0 85290 437 1

Typeset by Barnes Design + Print Group, Maidenhead
Printed and bound in Great Britain by Belmont Press, Northampton

CONTENTS

FOREWORD

Whatever the discipline or level of management, the responsibilities of managers are many and various. It is their job to produce results with essentially just two resources—people and time.

To maximise the potential of both, most managers need some reminders and basic guidelines to help them.

The Notes for Managers series provides succinct yet comprehensive coverage of key management issues and skills. The short time it takes to read each title will pay dividends in terms of utilising one of those key resources—people.

Selection interviewing is concerned with practical solutions to the problem of selecting the right person for a job. It is intended for line managers who are not personnel specialists, but who nonetheless find themselves involved in the often vexing problem of selection interviewing.

All too often, staff are taken on after only the most subjective and inaccurate examination of their suitability for the job. Failure to make the right decision not only produces costly staff turnover, but also jeopardises the efficiency of the whole organisation.

This booklet aims to give all the necessary guidelines to avoid this situation developing.

ALISTAIR GRAHAM
Director, The Industrial Society

I

SELECTION INTERVIEWING

INTRODUCTION

This booklet aims to help those who carry out selection interviews in order to select the right person for the right job. There are many aids to recruitment available in today's marketplace; psychometric testing, assessment centres etc.; some are tried and tested; others are still in experimental stages but most require the application of the necessary expertise in a specialist field. This can be a costly exercise, although many organisations would argue that it is a worthwhile investment when recruiting key staff. However, at present, there is no method which can provide a 100 per cent success rate or take away from the line manager the final responsibility for the selection decision.

Even when other selection methods are used, the interview plays a part in the whole process. This booklet is therefore concerned primarily with the interview itself and is written mainly for managers or supervisors, who are not personnel specialists but whose responsibility it is to interview from time to time.

Often the skill of interviewing is taken for granted and sometimes staff are employed after only the most subjective examination of their ability to suit the job. Failure to make the right choice not only produces costly staff turnover, but also jeopardises the efficiency of the whole organisation.

It is also worth remembering that the selection interview is a public relations exercise and if an organisation wishes to attract the best candidates, it needs to be seen to be fair and professional in the way that the selection process is carried out.

1

WHAT IS THE
SELECTION INTERVIEW?

Selection, as the word indicates, is the act of 'choosing'; in business terms, selection means choosing a person who will give both a department and the organisation as a whole the results that it needs from a particular job. Since selection is a two way process, it is equally important that in today's world, where expectations of work are higher than ever, the organisation is equally able to meet the aspirations of the individual. Any selection which does not give the organisation the results it needs is costing unnecessary money.

An equally important cost, though one more difficult to measure, is the effect that the wrong person in a job can have on other people. If an employee works as part of a team, then any inadequacies will affect the team, producing failures in their performance. Even if the employee works alone, these inadequacies will have an effect on the people with whom he or she comes into contact. The employee who is performing inadequately because he or she has been wrongly selected will also probably suffer loss of morale (and unnecessary stress as a result of this) along with the immediate manager who is trying to put right a situation that would, for all concerned, have been better avoided in the first place.

'Inadequacies,' of course, cannot be measured simply in terms of job performance. An employee might be highly skilled and capable at the job but if their attitude towards colleagues is destructive or un-cooperative it will upset the harmony that is essential to achieve the best results from people.

It is clear then that a manager must look closely at a person's experience, skills and characteristics before taking the major step of choosing that person for a job in the organisation.

2

LEGISLATION
AND DISCRIMINATION

More and more organisations are describing themselves as 'equal opportunities employers'. What does this mean? There is clearly a difference between good intentions and a realised policy which is not just about compliance with the law but improving and broadening the 'talent base' of an organisation and improving motivation, performance and results.

Although this booklet is about the selection interview (and equal opportunities clearly have much wider implications for working practices) there is no doubt that much of what the codes of practice recommend can be implemented through the selection process. Employers will obviously wish to avoid both direct and indirect discrimination in selection where it is illegal and this booklet aims to highlight the 'danger zones' where appropriate. However, the potential benefits of a pro-active policy with the commitment of senior management behind it are far greater than merely avoiding the tribunal courts.

There are many examples of equal opportunity policies, in both the public and private sectors, where management and employee relations have improved and where the problems of finding the right people for the right jobs have been tackled better. In this respect, equal opportunities are no longer a luxury and employers should consider how best they can implement a policy for their organisation. The Equal Opportunities Commission issues guidelines which can be used flexibly according to the size and needs of an organisation. Some employers will require less formal structures than others, while all employers will have to consider a time-scale against which they aim to achieve their objectives.

In this booklet, we will consider the implications of legislation and equal opportunities at each stage of the selection process.

In most organisations, employees, particularly at a senior level, are not appointed without at least a second interview; a second or third opinion is helpful. The role of the 'second interviewer' does need to be clear though—what are they looking for (as distinct from the first interviewer)? Do they have the right of veto! Is it their responsibility to make the final decision?

Action:

Clarify the interview procedure and aim to give the immediate line manager the responsibility for the final decision, even though other personnel specialists, senior management etc. may be involved in the procedure.

3

WHO SELECTS PEOPLE?

Most organisations today have a personnel department which specialises in a number of areas, one of which is selecting people for jobs. In some cases, this responsibility has passed completely from the line manager into the personnel specialist's hands. The results of this have been rather varied: at best the new employee's prospective manager sits in at some stage of the interview, or carries out an independent second interview which can be very satisfactory, or, at worst, the earliest the manager meets the new recruit is when he or she turns up for work on the first morning. As a result, the new employee may sometimes prove unable to do the job to the manager's satisfaction or be totally unsuitable as a person for the manager and the existing team. These problems could be avoided if the line manager and supervisor, where appropriate, were actively involved in the selection process, and encouraged to take responsibility for the decisions about the people working in the teams for which they are accountable.

Of course, the specialist skills of the personnel department are essential in establishing the recruitment process which is right for the organisation; attracting the right sort of candidates and sometimes picking out certain characteristics of a candidate that a non-specialist might miss. However, before a final decision is made, the manager in question should have the right to recommend the acceptance or rejection of a candidate, to be fair to the organisation and potential employee.

It is also true to say that many organisations, particularly in the public sector, select by panel or committee. These have both obvious advantages and disadvantages. Where senior public appointments are made for example, the board or committee are present to ensure fair play and a quality decision. However, this may not always be so if the panel are not properly briefed, or prepared, or its key members trained, in the selection process. Panels can be made up of a large number of interviewers and for a prospective junior employee to be faced with a panel of a dozen, or more, is obviously an intimidating experience which may not bring out the best in an interviewee.

4

HOW ARE PEOPLE SELECTED?

What is the normal chain of events that surrounds the selection of a new employee?

- A vacancy arises.
- What is the vacancy?
- Who should fill the vacancy?
- Where will we find the right person?
- How do we choose which person?
- The interview.
- Assessment.
- Placement.
- Follow-up.

In the sections that follow we will look more closely at each of these.

A vacancy arises

People resign from jobs for a reason. Sometimes that reason is unavoidable—retirement or ill-health, for example. Often the reasons are understandable and leave the organisation little choice in the short term—a better salary with another company is the obvious example here. At times, however, the reasons are such as to point to a failure in the organisation somewhere. Examples of these are dissatisfaction with job, prospects, or conditions; conflict with colleagues or boss; or a sense of injustice in the organisation.

If an employee is leaving because of the latter type of reason, then the organisation has a problem which must be looked into as soon as possible. For, if one person is affected in such a way the manager can be sure that others will be—and dissatisfied or disgruntled employees are costly, whether they leave the organisation or stay with it.

What can be done about this? The answer is to find out as quickly, and as accurately as possible, the reasons for people leaving by giving them a termination interview.

The timing of this interview is important. If it is held immediately the resignation is received, it may be possible to persuade the employee to stay (if that is what is wanted). Otherwise it is better to wait until the final day when they are more likely to tell the manager, or anyone else, what is really wrong.

Sometimes leavers prefer to deal with someone who is seen as neutral, so this termination interview is often done by the personnel officer. If this is the case, the manager must be sure to talk to the personnel officer afterwards to find out what points were made. Where possible, however, it makes sense for the personnel manager to do this interview.

For the termination interview to be of any real value leavers must be made to feel free to say whatever they think — without any defence or counter-arguments — and it must be guaranteed that everything said will be in confidence, certainly as far as colleagues and other employees are concerned. Finally, it is important that all employees see that action is taken to put right any faults of the organisation identified by this type of interview. But be warned—if the interview is as frank as it should be, personnel managers may sometimes hear things they don't like!

Sometimes the interview may reveal some problem with the organisation, or structure, which is making the leaver's job either too difficult, or too easy, or the person is too busy, or not busy enough. If this is the case it may well be that the manager should think seriously about the job, and whether it should exist at all or exist at least in a different form.

Action:

Ensure that all employees are interviewed and that the necessary steps are taken to put right the problems which the interview highlights.

What is the vacancy?

When a vacancy arises, it is an opportunity to reconsider overall functions and structure within a department. Does a job need to change, for example, to meet the changing needs and objectives of the organisation? Does the vacancy need to be filled at all, or is there a need to create a new function which did not exist previously?

There is always a danger that where managers have been very satisfied with a previous job-holder they will try to find an 'identikit' person to replace that job-holder. It is essential that managers think more broadly and the best way to do this is to begin by focusing on the job itself.

Therefore before managers can decide whether a job needs to be filled they have to know what the job actually is. This will require a job description.

The important questions that need to be answered in order to produce a job description are:

- What is the job title? (One that reflects the content of the job, and does not imply the sex of the job-holder.)
- Where is the job situated?
- Who will the job-holder be responsible to?
- What is the overall purpose of the job?
- What responsibilities does the job-holder have—for staff, materials, money? What are the consequences of any decisions in these areas?
- What are the key result areas of the job and the standards expected?
- With whom does the job-holder work?
- What are the terms and conditions of the job—hours, overtime, shifts, pay?
- What are the future career prospects, if any, for the holder of this job?

It is a good idea to get the answers to these questions from the present job-holder, if that person is available, as well as for the line manager to supply them. The two sets of answers will almost certainly be different, with the real facts lying some-where between the two. (If the answers produced by the job-holder and the boss are really different, this should be looked into in some depth—it probably means that in several areas of activity each of the two thinks that the other one is responsible for looking after it.) If the job-holder has actually left the company, attention should be paid to the comments made at that person's termination interview.

Action:

Establish the major aspects of the job. Look closely at the job—does it really need to be filled?

Who should fill the vacancy?

Having decided what the job is, the manager must then decide on the skills, attributes and experience required to carry out that job: i.e. a person specification. Care should be taken at this stage not to discriminate.

If the person specification is objectively based on the job description, rather than a prejudicial view of the sort of person 'one would like to see filling the job', discrimination is far less likely.

Person specifications are usually laid down under stan-dardised headings. There does not have to be a set format, although it may be helpful for an organisation to standardise its approach in order to ensure that the selection process is properly applied.

Again looking at the job itself, and considering the 'core' skills required to do that job, will point to the necessary cate-gories for the person specification.

The following headings may be useful. These are examples of the skills and attributes in specific areas that managers may consider:

1 Physical requirements

What standards of health and fitness are appropriate? Are there any points concerning vision, hearing dexterity etc? Ability to work under particular job conditions which are important?

Remember there is no point in putting restrictions on the type of candidate sought unless they are derived from the requirements of the job.

Consider if there are any physical aids or adaptions that could be used to employ a disabled person.

2 Education and training

General Education How relevant are specific academic requirements? Consider the job: does it require certain levels of literacy and numeracy rather than specific GCSE passes in Maths and English. The GCSEs may be helpful indicators but candidates may have achieved the required standards by some other means.

Specific Training For example vocational certificates, professional qualifications, apprenticeship certificates etc.

3 Experience

Should this be directly relevant or could similar experience in a different environment be considered?

Should length and breadth of experience be considered, level and range of responsibility, etc?

4 Special skills and knowledge

Specialist knowledge without which the job cannot be done —for example computer systems. How far does the job require particular aptitudes in understanding mechanical principles, dealing with figures, drawing skills etc? How will these be assessed at interview?

5 Personality and disposition

This is a difficult area, often vaguely defined, difficult to assess and most prone to bias at the interview. It is therefore more helpful to define personality traits as closely related to the job as possible. For example:

- *flexible:* (in terms of the job) someone who can easily adapt their previous arrangements to carry out a job in another part of the country with just half a day's notice.

- *outgoing:* (in terms of the job) someone who can listen to clients' needs and establish rapport with clients.

- *easy to get on with:* (in terms of the job) someone who can demonstrate that they have worked successfully as part of a team. Someone who is prepared to put their own work aside in order to help another member of the team with something urgent. Someone who is prepared to listen to and consider the views of others etc.

For each job it would be necessary to list the key 'disposition traits' and then to define each one if possible. It may be useful and objective to ask a range of current job-holders what they think those 'traits' might be before standardising the person specification.

6 Special circumstances

This should only form part of the specification where it is relevant to the job—for example travelling, staying away from home etc.

This can be a 'danger zone' for managers where questions are often asked in the form of 'Do you have any dependants?', 'Do you have children?' and so on. These questions can be directly discriminating if they are about the person and not the job. The question should be 'Are you able to travel and stay away from home?'

When compiling the specification, it may also be useful to state whether certain aspects are 'essential' or 'desirable'. The candidate who possesses all the desirable requirements as well as the essential ones will probably do the job particularly well, but sometimes these 'stars' are not available and a company may retain people longer if they are on an extended learning curve and necessary training can be provided. So, whilst we would insist that potential employees must meet the essential requirements, the desirable qualities are extras which may be helpful in assessing one candidate against another, but not a pre-requisite for the job.

When writing person specifications, it·is also tempting to describe the ideal and possibly unobtainable candidate. This may mean that potentially good candidates are eliminated and that recruits have high aspirations than can be met in the job.

Fitting a person to a realistic person specification will help to ensure that the job will be done well.

Action:

Produce a person specification based on realistic require-ments. Avoid discrimination. Be logical, specific and honest with yourself.

Where will we find the right person?

Employers need to think broadly about where to recruit if they are to attract a balanced group of applicants. When the job market is bouyant, it is also necesssary for managers to make recruitment a priority and to take advantage of opportunities to promote their organisation and form links with the local com-munity. It may be necessary to consider adjusting working practices, for example, flexible working hours, etc.—in order to attract a wider range of candidates.

Advertising in the national press is very expensive but there are alternative sources which can be considered, for example:

- internal advertisements
- external advertisements in
  - local press
  - specialist press
  - ethnic minority press
- employment agencies
- education and training establishments
- open evenings
- local community groups
- unsolicited sources
  - word of mouth
  - unsolicited letters
  - casual callers
  - recommendations from other employers or employees

Internal recruitment

As a matter of policy, most companies today notify their employees of vacancies. Some also use a vacancy as a training experience to develop staff. A few have an effective management development system linked to a realistic appraisal system which can produce the replacements virtually automatically. You can be fairly sure, however, that whatever method (or none) operates, there will be people within your organisation who at least deserve to be in the running for a vacancy. Not to make use of these people, if they do have the ability, is a major waste of resources and a sure way of demotivating staff. It is also a sure way of losing them—if they cannot obtain promotion within your organisation they are likely to go to one where they can.

Advertising

If you chose to advertise and have selected the appropriate publication on grounds of specialism, circulation within the community, level of vacancy, locality etc., it is worth considering the content of the advertisement.

A good agency will advise on the layout and presentation. Again remember that the advertisement promotes an image of the organisation. You need to consider the content and the following points may be helpful.

- The company
  - name
  - logo
  - what it does, size etc.
- The job
  - title
  - duties
  - location
- The person required
  - summarise the points from your person specification
- Benefits package
  - salary—phrases like 'salary negotiable' may be interpreted as meaning low salary

Action:

Check that your advertisement is not breaking the sex or race discrimination acts. Job advertisements should not state or imply that the job is only for applicants of one sex or race. Make sure the information is accurate, as the advertisement may form part of the contract between you and your new employee. Also consider including an equal opportunities statement to encourage a wider variety of applicants.

How do we choose which person?

Whatever method of attracting candidates you have chosen, you will now have a number of applicants. You are now going to work through the stages to the final acceptance of a candidate.

1 Application forms

Forms can present a professional image and are on the whole easier to pre-select from. A common format means that you are asking candidates for more easily comparable information. However, CVs are often used and do tend to speed up the recruitment process. There may also be certain cases where requiring applicants to complete application forms is an inhibiting factor and puts potentially good candidates off. Such potential employees should be encouraged to come direct to the company.

THE LEGAL STATUS OF FORMS

Although case law has not provided definite guidance, it can be assumed that forms are part of what, in the Sex Discrimination Act are described as 'arrangements made for deciding who should be offered employment'. (Section 6(i) (a)).

This means that some questions could be unlawful. Examples of such questions deal with family, ages of children, marital status etc. Some of the unfair beliefs which frequently influence judgement about the suitability of women for a job are, for example:

- women with children are unreliable
- women are more likely to have time off work owing to illness (particularly women's problems)
- women of marriageable age are interested in only short-term employment.

However each case must be considered in terms of its own particular facts. These cannot be elicited by questions on paper. There is no point, therefore, in asking questions which suggest 'stereotyping' and arouse suspicions of prejudice and discrimination.

INFORMATION FOR MONITORING PURPOSES

Where a monitoring procedure is carried out as part of an equal opportunites policy, the information which includes points about racial origin, marital status, and so on, is usually provided on a separate sheet, or tear-off slip, which is not made available to those making decisions at any stage of the selection process.

PRE-SELECTION

Unless candidates are attending an 'open day' or coming directly to the organisation, this is usually done by comparing the application form to the person specification. There are draw-backs to this because often information is incomplete and pre-selection may be carried out by someone fairly inexperienced in selection. It may be worthwhile involving line management and at least a second opinion at this stage. CVs can present problems because you are pre-selecting on the information candidates have chosen to give you rather than information common to all candidates that you need to have.

It is worth bearing in mind that even if candidates fail to meet the essential requirements for a particular job they may still be worth considering for another post in the organisation. On the other hand, it may mean that the type of candidate required is not available, the person specification over ambitious, or the advertising was not specific enough or was incorrectly placed. The decision must then be whether to re-advertise, or to retrain, or to take the 'best of those available'—often a vacancy is better left unfilled and temporary measures taken rather than to appoint the 'wrong' person out of desperation.

Action:

Use application forms where possible, unless it is a job which does not require one.

2 Acknowledgements

It is obviously important to acknowledge all applications immediately and let candidates know as soon as possible whether their application is to be progressed further or rejected.

Action:

Tell the candidate as soon as possible what is happening.

PREPARING THE CANDIDATE FOR INTERVIEW

It is worth deciding what information about the job and the organisation should be sent out before the interview. You may even do this prior to pre-selection when initial applications are made, not just to those short-listed for interview.

You will then present both a more professional image of the organisation and cut down on the amount of time spent giving information during the interview. You also help the candidate to make selection decisions about your job and your organisation: remember the interview is a two-way process.

SHORT-LISTING

It is difficult to prescribe how many candidates to interview; it may be that those pre-selected on the basis of person specification criteria constitute a large number. Much will depend on how many apply in the first place. Where there are large numbers, it is best to try and limit yourself on the basis of pre-selection but also to work through your list of 'less likely' candidates where necessary. It is probably better to see more candidates than less, although it is obviously a crucial factor. Consider the time well invested though if you select the right person—you must also allow enough time for each candidate that you see; too many in-depth interviews in one day may not help the interviewer or candidate.

Where the urgency to appoint and not to risk losing candidates through delay is a factor, it may be necessary to consider interviewing outside normal working hours.

The interview

Preparation before

Brief reception, and anyone else involved, and give the name of those expected for interview. If appropriate, arrange for a tour of the place of work. Sometimes informal discussions with other members of a department already doing the same or similar job may help candidates to form a more realistic picture of the job and organisation. It is also useful for candidates to meet those people they may be working with. There is little mileage to be gained in raising expectations too high: candidates need to understand as far as is possible the true nature of a job.

This means sometimes stressing the less attractive and more mundane aspects of a job—for example, being an air-steward is not about glamorous international travel.

The interview room

If a true picture of candidates is to be gained they must be made to feel as relaxed as possible. Provide a comfortable, private room for the interview with few, if any, distractions in or around it. Often an interviewer sits behind a desk, but this can very easily act as a psychological barrier between the interviewer and the candidate, and is certainly not likely to help the candidate relax. Sometimes it is better to have two fairly comfortable chairs with perhaps a small table next to them on which to rest notes and so on. However, some people find the lack of formality off-putting—judge each situation on its own merits.

The interviewer should try to ensure privacy by arranging for there to be no unnecessary interruptions and for telephone calls to be transferred elsewhere.

Planning the interview

Interviewers should look over the candidate's application form before the interview to familiarise themselves with the candidate's history, and, by comparing it with the person specification, to pick out the points that need to be investigated further.

With this and the person specification available, interviewers should then prepare a plan of how they want the interview to go in terms of areas to be explored. Of course, the actual interview will have to be flexible, according to the candidate, but a plan helps to systematically guide the interview through all the relevant areas missing out nothing of importance.

It is probably a good idea for interviewers to think of the sort of question they will begin with. The candidate is probably a little tense at the beginning so a neutral question tends to open the interview up without putting the candidate under any real pressure. A good topic, for example, would be to find out how the person travelled to the interview.

STRUCTURE

A useful structure may follow the categories selected for the person specification. Questions which are related to these categories should be prepared beforehand; these key questions, which are therefore relevant to the job, should be asked of each candidate. In this way, employers can demonstrate that they have treated candidates fairly, and assessing one candidate against another is more easily validated.

Obviously, the pursuit of these key questions will depend on probing, and following up, leads to individual answers given, as well as individual issues which arise from application forms.

It is also useful to plan information supplied, and to reserve this for the latter part of the interview, so that valuable time is not wasted talking about the job, instead of finding out about the candidate.

Finally, interviewers should make sure they have all the relevant papers, including information on terms and conditions, renumeration etc., that they are likely to need.

Objectives of the interview

It is important that interviewers are quite clear what their objectives are in an interview:

- to find out whether the candidate is suitable for the job and the organisation
- to find out whether the job and the organisation are suitable for the candidate
- to ensure that the candidates have a fair deal, thus developing a positive public image.

The importance of the first two cannot be over-emphasised: but while the importance of the candidate's suitability is fairly obvious, the question of the organisation's suitability for the candidate is often overlooked. Yet the commitment of candidates to an organisation and a job that suits them is crucial to its profitability and effectiveness.

Opening the interview

Having greeted the candidate, and checked the name (interviewers have been known to interview the wrong person), interviewers should introduce themselves, and offer the candidate a chair.

At this stage interviewers should then use their prepared opening question to break the ice. After that it is well worth telling the candidate that this is really a two-way situation. It is amazing how often candidates are surprised at being told that they are expected to gain information from the interviews as well as give it. It is a good idea to stress to candidates that they must feel free to ask questions whenever they are not sure of something.

Explain the structure and order of questions so that the candidate knows what to expect.

Interviewers should ask if the candidate objects to them taking notes—purely as reminders of the more important facts in the interview. The notes themselves should be short phrases, often trigger-words, to remind the interviewer to return to a point later, or to help summarise at the end. A useful tip is for the interviewer not to make a note immediately after candidates say something which could be a point against themselves, but to wait until the conversation has moved on to another topic.

Action:

Put the candidate at ease. Tell the person what the interview is trying to achieve. Get agreement to the taking of notes.

What to do in the interview

Using the prepared plan and the person specification, interviewers should make sure they work steadily through all the relevant areas, collecting facts and opinions (of the candidates) as they go along. It is up to interviewers to make sure they have got all the facts they need, and that they are complete and correct. It will be too late after the interview has finished!

Certainly it is important that the interviewer probes the apparent facts. For example, it is not enough to note that a candidate was a supervisor in his or her previous job. How many people were supervised? In what jobs? What were the actual responsibilities of the supervisor? In other words, what do the facts really mean?

Action:

Get all the correct facts required. Probe these facts to obtain the details behind them. Supply necessary information about the job and ensure the candidate has the opportunity at the end to ask questions or supply relevant additional information.

The interviewer's skills

If interviewers are to form a realistic picture of a candidate they must get the candidate to talk. A sure way of failing to do that is by asking 'yes-no' questions. Instead the interviewer ought to ask open-ended questions that force the candidate to give wider and more complex replies. For example, the question 'Did you enjoy your last job?' gets the answer 'Yes' or 'No'— and that won't really tell the interviewer much. On the other hand, the question 'What did you think of your last job?'

requires candidates to express their own opinions in their own way, which is far more valuable to the interviewer. Open-ended questions usually start with 'How', 'What', 'Why', 'When', or 'Where'—try to use these whenever possible. Such questions will lead to other—probably more specific—questions.

Often the best way to assess a person's future performance is to gather evidence about their past performance. In addition to open questions which get candidates talking, the so-called 'behavioural' question is a way of exploring what people have actually done in areas relevant to the job. They may be questions which start off 'closed' to establish a specific fact and then a follow-up 'open' question is asked to explore the facts. They may begin with phrases like:

'Give me an example of a time when you have had to do. . .'
'In what circumstances did you have to make a quick decision . . .'
'What did you do in your last job to contribute towards team-work. Be specific . . .'
'Give me an instance when in your last job, you had to let others know how you thought or felt . . .'

Hypothetical questions—the 'what would you do if . . .?' variety are often used but can be unrealistic and discriminatory if the hypothetical situation is totally outside the candidate's experience. Use this type with care. Information supplied through behavioural questioning is probably a more objective frame of reference on which to base decisions.

It is also important to give candidates time to think of their answers and to summarise throughout, both to clarify mis-understandings and to keep the interview on course.

Often the candidate, for a number of reasons, will leave out facts or bend them to suit the situation. If interviewers are concentrating on listening to and observing the candidate, they will pick up clues to these situations and can then explore them in more depth. It is enormously important that the interviewer listens closely to what is being said and actively observes the manner in which it is being said. Nervousness when answering particular questions may possibly be a sign of extra tension caused by telling a half-truth or even a lie.

The other advantage of the interviewer concentrating on the candidate is that it impresses on the person their importance to the interviewer and to the company. A candidate in that position is far more likely to really open up, with obvious benefits to the interviewer.

Action:

Ask open-ended questions and behavioural questions. Listen to what the candidate says. Watch what candidates do and how they react to questions. Summarise throughout.

Pressures during the interview

There are pressures on the candidate throughout the interview. It is the interviewer's job to minimise these in order to achieve the frame of mind in the candidate that will allow the person to talk freely and objectively.

There are all sorts of stories about 'stress' interviews—bright lights or direct sunshine, tall chairs, aggressive questions. For the selection interview, the interviewer should concentrate on reducing stress not producing it.

Objectivity has already been mentioned in relation to the candidate. It is impossible for candidates to be completely objective about themselves and in the same way good interviewers should recognise that they, too, are unable to be totally objective, unless a really big effort is made to recognise and accept these failings and compensate for them when interviewing. The interviewer should particularly watch out for positive and negative bias toward a candidate. An example of positive bias would be the subconscious assumption that the candidate was a 'good person' because he or she came from the same town, or went to the same school, or played the same sport as the interviewer.

Equally, something that irritates the interviewer—colour of hair or skin, sex, background, accent—could produce a subconscious dislike of the candidate, a feeling that the person could not really do the job properly. Either feeling is dangerous to interviewers. Their job is to obtain the facts about a person and to compare them — objectively — with the requirements in the specification.

Only after that has been done should judgement come into it. And even then it should be an honest judgement uninfluenced by the interviewer's own personal likes and dislikes. Interviewers who say they can tell straight away 'just by looking at them' whether people will be right for a job or not, are doing themselves, their company, and the candidate a grave disservice.

One way to test one's subconscious prejudices is to seek alternative evidence. If you have very positive feelings about an issue or aspect of a candidate, test or try out the negative or opposite aspects of the same issue and *vice versa*—in other words, seek contrary evidence, whether positive or negative.

Gut feelings cannot and probably should not be ignored. However, they should be 'pushed aside' during the interview and not permit a premature decision to be made ten minutes after the interview has begun. If you have doubts and suspicions, it pays to be honest and open with candidates so that they have every opportunity to allay your fears. Your honesty may even help them to realise that they may be making a wrong decision about the job which is also in your interests.

You may reflect upon your feelings after the interview when you have the facts before you and perhaps the benefit of a second interview and another opinion.

Action:

Remove as much stress from the interview as is possible.

Finishing the interview

When interviewers have got all they need from the interview, they should check that the candidate has no further questions and then signify the end of the interview.

They should:

- check that the candidate's expenses were covered if this is policy

- tell the candidate what will happen next, i.e. offering the job, rejecting the applicant (explaining why), or telling the person when to expect a decision, or second interview
- thank the candidate for coming and see the person out.

Action:

End the interview firmly. Tell the candidate what to expect next.

Assessment after the interview

The decision

Now interviewers come to the often difficult process of matching what they know of the candidate against what they want (the person specification). This is a difficult task, and it must be done carefully and honestly; mistakes are expensive and a company of any repute realises that it has a moral responsibility to the candidate, as well as to itself, to make as correct a decision as possible.

One of the best ways of reaching a decision is for the interviewer to work steadily through the person specification giving the candidate a rating against each part of the following scale:

A = much above average — 150 per cent
B = above average — 125 per cent
C = average — 100 per cent
D = below average — 75 per cent
E = much below average — 50 per cent

The ideal candidate for the job (bearing in mind that the person specification prescribes the person who will do the job satisfactorily) will have all Cs. Anyone with As or Es is probably too good, or bad, for the particular job. Someone with Bs is probably acceptable if there is a foreseeable move for them in twelve months' time or so. Someone with Ds will require some training.

Weighting

Very often one of the factors (e.g. training) will be of particular importance. Decide this when the person specification is being drawn up to avoid bias after the interview. The effect of this extra importance is to weight the decision. For example, if training is important and the candidate is rated C on that point, one other C plus three Ds should be enough to lift the overall rating to a C, thus making the candidate acceptable.

Another useful technique that the interviewer can employ to help with the decision is to visualise the candidate in typical situations that the job will provide and to consider how the person might get on. (E.g. how would the candidate cope with Bert Jones when Bert's machine goes down for the third time in a day?)

Many companies use a standard interview assessment form. This requires interviewers to put down their own comments, assessments and decisions under various headings. The value of this is that it allows one candidate to be compared against another fairly objectively (this is particularly valuable if one candidate was seen at 9.30 on Tuesday and the next at 3.15 on Thursday).

When the decision has been made, particularly if it is to reject the candidate, the interviewer should make sure that the record of the outline of the interview includes why the candidate was rejected. If a rejected candidate alleges discrimination because of race, union activities, sex, or against rehabilitating certain offenders, it is up to the company concerned to prove its innocence. Records of the decision and the reasons behind it are highly valuable in this situation.

Action:

Assess the facts. Keep a record of the interview.

The offer of employment

If the decision is made to offer the job to the candidate, it is normally made subject to a satisfactory medical examination and references. (Also the contract should contain all the aspects required by the Employment Protection (Consolidation) Act 1978.)

References are always a problem. Testimonials brought by the candidate to the interview should be viewed with great suspicion unless the interviewer can verify them with the company concerned.

The normal type of written reference from a company is a wordy statement about a candidate's moral integrity and so on—not very helpful at all. The interviewer can improve on this considerably by writing to the referee asking specific questions, such as:

'What are the dates between which Mr/Ms . . . worked for you?'
'What was the job title?'
'What did it involve?'
'What was the rate of pay?'
'How many day's sickness did the person have in the last two years?'

and the clincher

'Would you re-employ the person?'

Some companies will refuse to answer some or all of these. Of those who do, a favourable reference should not carry a great deal of weight with the interviewer, whereas, on the other hand, an unfavourable one obviously deserves further investigation.

Action:

Make it clear that the offer is subject to satisfactory medical examination and references. Look particularly at poor references.

Placement

Once the candidate has accepted the offer of employment, and the medical and references are satisfactory, the line manager should take steps to make sure that the new employee will be properly received on the first day, and given induction training and whatever job training is necessary to make the person an effective member of the organisation as soon as possible.

Remember induction begins once a future employee has been made a job offer.

Action:

Plan the induction and the training of the new employee.

Follow-up

When the employee has been fully inducted and has properly settled in, the manager should stand back and take a long hard look at the months passed since that person was appointed to see if the employee is really what the interviewer thought he or she would be at the interview. If the person is not, what aspects were missed or wrongly interpreted at the interview, and what can the interviewer do to try to avoid the same mistake next time? In the short term this will show up in appraisal interviews, but eventually the termination interview will have very good feedback also on the validity of the choice.

Action:

Was it the right decision?

II

APPENDICES

APPENDIX 1

SELECTION INTERVIEW — CHECKLIST

1 Purpose

To match a person to a job.

2 Preparation

- Study available data, e.g. job description, person specification, school report, application form, test results etc.
- Make an interview plan — guard against bias.
- Allow adequate time.
- Ensure privacy — ensure room appropriate to job ranking — no interruptions.
- Ensure proper reception of applicant.

3 Conduct

- Put at ease, welcome in a friendly way (don't keep applicant waiting).
- Be sure to give precise details about the job concerned.
- Encourage applicant to talk freely about previous jobs, interests etc. Do this by the type of question used. Don't ask leading questions or those which only require a 'yes' or 'no' answer.
- Listen and observe.
- Check that all relevant ground is covered.
- Advise when an answer can be expected.

4 Follow up

- Decide on suitability of applicant — guard against bias.
- Advise accordingly.

APPENDIX 2

TERMINATION INTERVIEW — CHECKLIST

1 Purpose

(a) To discover person's true reasons for leaving the company with a view to taking any required action to prevent others leaving for the same reasons. Such reasons could be in respect of:

- poor recruitment
- selection
- inadequate training
- company policy
- salary
- management/supervision.

(b) To secure employee's goodwill and company's reputation.

2 Preparation

- Check resignation letter — reason stated.
- Study employee's records.
- Where necessary check with other appropriate people, e.g. supervisor, etc.
- Ensure privacy and no interruptions.
- Allow adequate time.

3 Conduct

- Put at ease.
- State purpose of interview.
- Encourage and allow employee to talk freely about the job, the company and the people.
- Listen and observe: be alert for clues to underlying reason.
- Thank employee for services rendered and wish him or her well.

4 Follow-up

Decide if any action is necessary in the light of information gained, and implement accordingly.

APPENDIX 3

GUIDE TO EMPLOYMENT LEGISLATION

The main Acts relating to employment are:

Race Relations 1976; Sex Discrimination 1975; Sex Discrimination Act 1986; Equal Pay 1970; Equal Value (Amendment) Regulations, 1983; Disabled Persons 1944, 1958.

These acts seek to promote equality of opportunity and to ensure that no person is treated less favourably than another person, simply on the grounds of their race, nationality, colour, ethnic origin, sex or disability. Under the acts it is unlawful for employers to discriminate in recruitment, promotion, training or transfer, terms and conditions of employment and dismissal. Employers are also liable for unlawful discriminatory acts carried out by their employees in the course of their employment, unless they can show that they took such steps as were reasonably practicable to prevent them from occurring. Job applicants or employees who believe they have suffered discrimination may take their complaint to an Industrial Tribunal.

Discrimination

The most common types of discrimination are:

- *Direct discrimination*—consists of treating a person less favourably than others
- *Indirect discrimination*—consists of applying a requirement or condition which, whether intentional or not, adversely affects one group rather than another.

Both direct and indirect discrimination are unlawful. The acts apply to all employers, their employees and to all employment agencies.

Exceptions to this are in cases of genuine occupation qualification. For *race relations* these are where:

1 If authenticity is required for a dramatic performance, or as a model, or where there is desire for a 'special ambience' where food or drink is served.

2   Where the job-holder provides services and welfare, and those services can be provided most effectively by a person of that racial group. This applies to welfare, social services etc., and explains why advertisements for 'Bengali waiter' are allowed under the acts.
   For sex discrimination they are where:

1   As (1) above.
2   Where the job involves physical contact with the opposite sex, or working in a place where members of the opposite sex are likely to be in a state of undress — for example lavatory attendants and persons who sell clothes and may assist in changing rooms.
3   Work in single sex prisons, hospitals etc.
4   Where the law requires the employee to be of a particular sex.
5   The job involves working outside the UK in a country whose laws and customs are such that the duties could not effectively be performed by a person of the opposite sex.
6   Different height requirements for male and female prison officers and police.
7   Ministers of Religion.
8   The Armed Forces.

The Commission for Racial Equality and the Equal Opportunities Commission promote a *code of practice* to implement equal opportunities policies. The codes of practice do not have the force of the law, but employers who do follow the codes of practice are more likely to ensure they follow the spirit of the acts and are less likely to discriminate unwittingly (indirectly). The codes of practice embody the practical steps employers need to take to move towards equality of opportunity:

● responsibility for the policy should be allocated to a suitably qualified member of senior management
● the extent and implementation of the policy should be discussed and agreed with trade unions and employee representatives
● the policy should be made known to all employees and job applicants
● training and guidance on the law and company policy should be provided for supervisory staff and other relevant decision-makers
● selection procedures and criteria should be examined for indirect discriminatory effects and charged where this is found
● the policy should be monitored through analysis of the ethnic origins and gender of the workforce and job applicants.

Monitoring and review

Through monitoring and gathering statistical data on the shape of the workforce, employers can identify areas of under-representation. Appropriate action can then be taken.

Positive action should not be confused with positive discrimination. Positive discrimination means employing someone simply because of their race, sex etc. This is illegal in this country. Positive action is the term used for measures taken under Section 37 and 38 of the Race Relations Act and under 7.10 − 7.20 of the Sex Discrimination Act, which in broad terms enables employers, training bodies and trade unions to:

- encourage applications for job or membership from members of a particular racial group or sex
- provide training to help fit them for particular work or posts where they are under-represented.

These exceptions do not however make it lawful for the employer to discriminate at the point of selection to achieve a balance of gender or race

Segregation The Race Relations Act states that to separate a person from other persons on racial grounds is seen as less favourable treatment, even if the facilities are equal or better.

Disabled Persons (Employment) Act 1944

The act provides that every employer with 20 or more employees has a duty to employ a quota of registered disabled people. The quota is currently 3 per cent of the workforce.

An employer who is below quota should not engage anyone other than a registered disabled person without first obtaining a permit to do so.

The jobs of lift attendant and car park attendant have been designated for registered disabled people.

Equal Pay Act 1970

The main act came into force in December 1975 and the Equal Pay (Amendment) Regulations 1983 on 1st January 1984.

Scope of the act

The title of the act is misleading as it covers almost all the contractual conditions of service and is not restricted to pay. It gives women the right to an 'equality clause' which means that if any term in their contract is less favourable than that in a man's contract it can be modified to make it the same. Also if there is a clause in a man's contract giving him some benefit which is not in the woman's contract it will be awarded to the woman.

A man is also entitled to equality with a woman.

Who can claim

Men and women are entitled to equal pay and conditions if:

1 they are employed on 'like work', which means that their work is the same or of a broadly similar nature,
2 their jobs have been given equivalent rating under a non-discriminatory job evaluation scheme,
3 if paragraphs (1) and (2) do not apply, if their work is of 'equal value' in terms of the demands made on them (for instance under such headings as effort, skill and decisions).

A woman may establish that her work is similar to a man's under one of these three headings, but she will not be entitled to equal pay if the employer can show that the variation in pay is due to a "material difference (other than the difference of sex) between her case and his".

Enforcement of the act

A claim may be made to an industrial tribunal during the period of employment or within six months of leaving. A woman can only claim parity with a fellow male employee and a man with a female employee.

If the claim is successful the tribunal can award the difference in pay between the claimant and the employee selected as the comparator backdated for up to two years before the date when the proceedings were instituted.

This appendix is merely a guide to the acts. The law is interpretive; for a particular query or situation, the following bodies will be able to offer further information:

Commission for Racial Equality
Elliot House
10-12 Allington Street
London SW1E SEH

Equal Opportunities Commission
Overseas House
Quay Street
Manchester M3 3AN
Tel: 061-833 9244

Both provide a range of publications and guides to the acts.

The Industrial Society
Peter Runge House
3 Carlton House Terrace
London SW1
Tel: 01-839 4300

The Industrial Society has a phone-in information service which deals
with any matter relating to employment legislation. All enquiries are
treated confidentially.

APPENDIX 4

THE BOARD OR PANEL INTERVIEW

Advantages

1   Reduces the bias inherent in the individual interview.
2   Enables different interests to be represented so that candidates are viewed from several aspects.
3   Gives each member a chance to concentrate wholly on listening to the candidate while others are asking questions.
4   Makes a more impressive occasion suitable for senior appointments.
5   Enables inexperienced interviewers to learn from experienced ones.

Disadvantages

1   Takes a great deal of time to organise and involves a lot of highly paid manpower.
2   Creates a formal atmosphere which inhibits some candidates.
3   While it overcomes individual bias, it sometimes creates other problems due to serious differences and disagreements between Board members.

Constitution

Sometimes as many as 20 (generally too large to be effective); three or at the most five is appropriate for industry/commerce. This allows for variety in membership (e.g. status, technical or other interest, sex, age, etc.). It enables all members to participate and share the work of interviewing and assessing.

The chairperson

Usually the senior person in the group or someone in a neutral situation, e.g. the personnel or staff officer. He or she should be someone with a wide knowledge of the company and the jobs available.

The chairperson is responsible for:

- planning the work of the board
- briefing members of the board of requirements of the job and the main points of each candidate
- greeting the candidate, introducing members
- opening the interview with 'formal' questions such as verifying basic details of the job and the candidate
- possibly calling on other members to question the candidate or give further information about the job
- closing the interview and telling the candidate when they can expect to hear the results
- thanking the candidate for attending.

The chairperson conducts the assessment by inviting and summing up opinions of members and formulating an agreed view. As in any office, the chairperson is in control of the proceedings and gets to know the idiosyncrasies of his or her members and how to deal with them tactfully.

Members

Members of the board share the questioning and information—given according to a pre-arranged plan. When not asking questions etc., they must listen to and observe the candidate and make their own assessments. They should avoid repeating questions or comments made by other members, unless seriously dissatisfied with candidate's replies. During the assessment they should state their own opinion and discuss it.

Planning and procedure

Careful planning is essential to avoid wasting time and also to enable the board to give a business-like impression. They should have a plan of campaign and stick to it. For example, a three member panel or board might work as follows:

1   The chairperson welcomes the candidate and introduces members, checks main particulars of job and candidate, and may ask further questions on some specific topic.
2   Technical members may ask questions on technical qualifications and experience.
3   'User Department' (i.e. probably candidate's future boss) asks further questions on type of experience, background, interests, etc.

4 Chairperson asks further information, gathering questions and makes sure candidate has asked all the questions and got all information he or she needs. The chairperson then concludes the interview.

Timing: ten minutes for chairperson, five minutes each member. This may be taken in order — or varied — but too much hopping about confuses both candidate and panel members. The chairperson must make sure all points have been covered (some kind of checklist may be helpful).

Assessment

This may be done by informal discussion of members' overall impressions of the candidate or, more generally, by some rating sheet. A five-point scale (giving two points discrimination above and below average) is a sound basis. This may be an alphabetical or numerical scale — depending on the basis of assessment (e.g. NIIP seven-point-plan) — so various aspects of the job must be 'weighed up'. For example, experience will probably be more important than health and physique. Members mark their own rating sheets and then the chairperson invites comments from members, giving ample opportunity for discussing varying views. As the chairperson is usually a senior person, his or her views should be stated last or they may unduly influence ratings of individual members. Agreement may be reached by informal discussion or by a vote; if agreement is impossible the chairperson usually has the casting vote. While selection is a great responsibility for all the board members, the wise chairperson will usually be influenced by the wishes of the user department.

Assessment may take place immediately after each interview and while it is obviously advantageous to rate each candidate while they are fresh in mind, there are disadvantages to this in that it takes time (a lot of time if serious differences exist). This sometimes leads to an acrimonious discussion, leaving panel members bad-tempered and irritable and acts unfavourably on the following candidate. It is generally better to allow members just time to mark their own rating sheet and note special points they wish to raise on each available candidate. All candidates are assessed at the end; where only one job is available, candidates are ranked in order of preference.

General

As in all selection interviews, the candidate must be treated courteously and an effort should be made to make the interview as friendly and informal as possible: this is more difficult to achieve within the formal setting of a board interview. Board members need some training in interviewing and in the use of the rating sheet and any other 'aids'—and the chairperson and members must learn to work together as a team.